PUFFIN'S HOMECOMING

The Story of an Atlantic Puffin

SMITHSONIAN
WILD HERITAGE COLLECTION

To my parents, David and Jeanette Goldstein
— *D.B.*

To Morgan
— *K.L.*

Copyright © 1993 by Trudy Management Corporation,
165 Water Street, Norwalk, CT 06856, and Smithsonian Institution,
Washington, DC 20560.

10 9 8 7 6 5 4 3 2
Printed in Singapore

Library of Congress Cataloging-in-Publication Data

Bailer, Darice.

Puffin's homecoming : the story of an Atlantic puffin / by Darice Bailer :
illustrated by Katie Lee.
        p.   cm.
Summary: Follows the activities of an Atlantic Puffin as he returns to the island
where he was born, meets his mate, and raises a lively chick.
      ISBN 0-924483-90-3
1. Atlantic puffin — Juvenile fiction. [1. Puffins — Fiction.]
I. Lee, Katie. 1942-　ill. II. Title.
      PZ10.3.B149Pu 1993   92-43762
      (Fic) — dc20   CIP
                                               AC

PUFFIN'S HOMECOMING

The Story of an Atlantic Puffin

by Darice Bailer

Illustrated by Katie Lee

Soundprints

A Division of Trudy Management Corporation
Norwalk, Connecticut

Alone, far out in the North Atlantic, Puffin drifts
and dives, floats and flies. He lives at sea through
seven cold and stormy months. Then, as winter ends,
he grows restless. Spring is tugging him back again
toward the island where he was born.

Puffin's face is changing. His large, triangular beak grows even bigger and is now etched bright orange-red and gold. Yellow rosettes decorate the corners of his mouth. Red-rimmed eyes are adorned with ornaments above and below, and sooty lines sweep back across white cheeks. He is becoming as colorful as a rainbow!

Orange webbed feet paddle steadily. At last Puffin sees the island's rocky cliffs rising from the sea.

He stops to preen. Rolling this way and that in the water, he can reach every glossy feather. A final feather is twitched into place while he is lying on his back!

Puffin becomes hungry. He dives and clamps
his beak tightly on a sand eel. Holding the
fish to the roof of his mouth with his
strong tongue, he tries for another.
Puffin brings *three* to the surface
and gobbles them quickly.

A black-backed gull is circling overhead looking for a meal. Alarmed, Puffin plunges to safety below the water. The gull cannot follow.

Puffin comes up for air near a pair of puffins.
"Clackety-clack-clack," they playfully rap their
bright beaks together. Puffin tries to join the fun,
but he is shooed away.

Skittering across the water, wildly flapping his small wings, Puffin clumsily takes off. Up he flies toward the cliff top. Then he slows his beating wings and pushes his big feet forward, using them as brakes. Just as he drops out of the sky, a sudden gust of wind tumbles him end over end.

Puffin rights himself near a burrow. It is the same rabbit hole that he and his mate use every summer. A head pokes out. For the first time in seven months, Puffin sees his mate! He bobs forward, and they wag their heads. They greet one another by noisily tapping beaks.

Then they get to work. They
have a three-foot-deep burrow
to clean. Scraping with claws,
shoveling and pushing with big
feet, Puffin and his mate are soon
covered from top to bottom with dirt.
Then feathers and bits of grass and seaweed
are gathered for the nest site deep within.

Many puffins now crowd the cliff top and dot the water below. Pairs work on their burrows and strut in front to warn others away.

Younger puffins come. They gather seaweed and grass, too. But they let the wind carry their bits away for they do not have burrows yet.

It is late in April when Puffin's
mate lays one large white egg.
She and Puffin take turns keeping
it warm. While one of them tucks the
egg under its breast feathers, the other stands
guard or flies to the sea for food.

23

After 40 days, a little chick pecks
her way out of the egg. Covered with
dark, soft down, her eyes are open and
she quickly stands.

Puffin and his mate are good parents. While
one guards the chick, the other brings her sand
eels and herring and other good things to eat.

Each parent can carry as many as 22 fish at one time! And the hungry chick grows fast, eating as much as half her weight in fish in a single day.

When not eating
or resting, the chick keeps busy.
She flaps her wings and parades up
and down. Digging and pushing with
her feet, she moves dirt from one side
of the burrow to the other — and then back again.
She tugs at roots growing through the roof. Stones
and twigs are picked up eagerly in her beak — then
dropped. They do not taste like fish!

The chick grows bigger and stronger. Then, one dark night in July, she scuttles outside the burrow for the first time. Waddling clumsily toward the ocean, she doesn't stop, not even at the cliff's edge. She tumbles right over — then sails and flutters, flapping her stubby wings hard. At last she flops into the water below.

And away she paddles. Completely at home in the sea, the chick will not touch land again for at least two years!

Puffin and his mate leave, too. Their summer job is finished. As their bright, springtime colors fade, they go their separate ways far out in the ocean. But they will meet again next year when once again spring pulls them back to their island home.

About the Atlantic Puffin

These small, stocky, sea birds (often called "sea parrots" by Arctic fishermen) are members of the Auk family and live off the rocky northern coastlines of North America and Europe. They spend their lives at sea, returning to land only to breed in the spring. Their single egg is laid in burrows or rock crevices where they faithfully tend their young until late July when the plump chicks are ready to care for themselves. Atlantic puffins wear bright colors during the breeding season, but appear somewhat drab during the rest of the year.

Glossary

beak: sharp, rigid, projecting mouth structure.

black-backed gull: a black-and-white sea bird with large wings and webbed feet. Black feathers mark its wings and back.

burrow: a hole in the ground, dug by an animal for shelter.

herring: a food fish that is abundant in the North Atlantic, sometimes canned and sold as sardines.

mate: either one of a breeding pair of animals.

North Atlantic: the Atlantic Ocean between Canada and northern Europe.

ornament: decoration, adornment.

rosette: gathered or pleated material with a decorative appearance.

sand eel: a small, elongated fish.

seaweed: plants that grow in the sea.

Points of Interest in this Book

p. 11 Puffins use wings to "fly" underwater, steering with their feet.

p. 12 Black-backed gulls prey on puffins.

p. 14 Because of their relatively heavy body weight and short wings, puffins must work hard at flying and may seem clumsy when they land.

pp. 16-17 Not only do puffins return to the same cliff every year, they return to the very same burrow.

pp. 20-21 Young puffins return to the cliffs of the breeding colony later than mature, mated pairs and may find all burrows occupied. They collect nesting materials, however, in imitation of the behavior of the mature birds.

p. 27 Feathers are growing through the young chick's down and will eventually replace it.

p. 28 The chick is almost full grown, but has a much smaller beak than its parents.